Framework for a General Theory of Cognition and Choice

Framework for a General Theory of Cognition and Choice

ROBERT M. AXELROD

Institute of International Studies
University of California, Berkeley

Standard Book Number 87725-118-5
Library of Congress Card Number 72-619609
© 1972 by the Regents of the University of California

PREFACE

The work reflected in this paper began with a concern
for the problems of strategy in international relations. While
studying strategic policy and the decision-making process, I
was struck over and over again by how much a person's decisions
will be affected by the way he understands the past. The "les-
son of Munich" is only one among many common examples. Therefore I undertook several studies of the process by which lessons
are learned by foreign policy decision-makers. These studies
(of the Military Assistance Program, 1965-67, and the Bay of
Pigs, 1961) never seemed satisfactory to me. The assumption
that conclusions are drawn from single events was valid in part,
but it was not adequate in itself. I was forced to think about
the more general question of how people use experience to form
and reform their beliefs. When applying this formulation to
international politics I kept running into another problem. The
problem is that there does not seem to be any justifiable way
to form or reform a belief under the conditions actually found
in international politics. Too much is known and—simultaneous-
ly—too little is known. For example, everyone knows that a
great many factors need to be taken into account for even a
limited understanding of the causes of war. Even policy-makers
do not seem to have enough direct or indirect experience to
choose between the many competing theories concerning war. Yet
policy-makers make policy. Baffled by this, I decided to move
back from the domain of decision-making into the domain of
cognition. After reading some of the major normative and empirical literatures of cognition, I was left with a collection
of theoretical approaches and a pile of experimental results.
I decided that what I wanted was a way of putting all the pieces
together so that I could move back and forth between cognition
and strategy. Putting such different pieces together would
require a mathematical model, and a highly abstract one at that.
The model would, in effect, be a general theory of cognition
and choice. And here it is. (Or here, at least, is an outline
of it.)

Of course, this reconstructed logic is a vast oversim-
plification of the "reasoning" that brought me to work on a
general theory. For a more accurate account, one could consult
with those who bore with me during the confusion: Hayward Alker,

PREFACE

Steven Brams, Matthew Bonham, Ernst Haas, Martin Landau, Nicholas Miller, Nelson Polsby, Michael Shapiro, Paul Sniderman, Michael Taylor, Aaron Wildavsky, and Zoltan Domotor. I owe them many thanks. To add that they are not responsible for the errors in this paper is an understatement. I also wish to express my thanks to those institutions whose collective faith was expressed in terms of financial support: the Institute of International Studies and the Committee on Research, both of the University of California at Berkeley.

R. M. A.

CONTENTS

CONTENTS

CONTENTS

INTRODUCTION

Purpose

This paper presents an outline of a general theory of cognition and choice. The purpose of the general theory is to encompass as many different social science literatures as possible in a single mathematical model. The mathematical model should be as elegant as possible. Elegance in mathematics is simplicity combined with power.

The theme of the paper is that many of the same aspects of cognition and choice problems have been studied under different labels in different literatures and that these various studies can be related to each other in the context of a mathematical model. The value of constructing the model is to help us understand the relationships between these separate literatures, and thereby be in a better position to reach new insights into the nature of the general cognition and choice problems and their separate parts. This paper merely begins this task.*

The theory being advanced is so abstract as to be practically devoid of substantive content. In effect it provides a formal language to treat a variety of specific substantive problems. Like other formal languages, its goal is not only to help communication but also to facilitate thought about a range of problems. In the case of the present theory, statements about cognition and choice are relatively easy to handle, but statements about personality and psychic needs are not. Within the realms of cognition and choice, the present framework is designed to handle the structural relationships among a set of specific beliefs.

The model is divided into six phases to represent a cumulative sequence of mathematical power. Each phase builds upon the preceding one and adds new material. The phases are named after the types of persons they are descriptive of. Thus, for example, the first phase is "believer" because it describes a person with a set of beliefs, but very little else.

---

*For an empirical application of some parts of this model, see Axelrod (forthcoming).

1

FRAMEWORK FOR A GENERAL THEORY OF COGNITION AND CHOICE

Outline

Table 1 provides an overview of the six phases of the model. Listed within each phase are the literatures that can be treated in terms of the model as it is developed in that phase. The literatures are divided into normative and empirical categories because some literatures deal primarily with how a person should think and act and other literatures deal with how people do in fact think and act.

Table 1

OVERVIEW OF THE MODEL

Phase	Normative Literatures	Empirical Literatures
1. Believer	Linear logic (arithmetic) Binary logic (Aristotelian)	Psycho-logic Cognitive consistency Concept formation
2. Observer	Data theory Information theory	S-R learning (passive) Channel capacity
3. Predictor	Regression Causal inference Epistemology	Closest point estimation (lessons of history)
4. Experimenter	Experimental design	S-R learning (active)
5. Decision-maker	Utility theory Decision-making under risk Bayesian inference	Satisficing Selective attention to goals Cognitive dissonance (after decision)
6. Strategist	Formal game theory	Experimental games

Types of Statements

Several distinct types of statements will be used that should be explained at the outset. (1) There are statements about primitives and the properties these primitives are assumed to possess; these statements are axioms. The primitives are the basic elements of the mathematical model. In Phase 1 two primitives are introduced: variables and beliefs. In Phase 3 another

2

primitive is introduced: prediction processes. All other formal terms are (I hope) expressible using these three basic terms. (2) There are statements expressing new terms using only old terms; these are definitions. (3) There are also a few simple theorems, which are statements that can be proved using the axioms and the definitions.

There are also three less formal types of statements. One is the coordinating definition, which tells what in the external world is meant by a formal term. A coordinating definition has no standing in the formal model. If someone else wants to give different coordinating definitions to some of the terms, that is fine. The mathematical model remains unchanged, and all the theorems are still valid. The coordinating definitions which I use are usually written in the form "X can be thought of as representing . . . ." Finally, there are hypotheses and conjectures. These are empirical claims about the way the external world actually operates. The hypotheses are statements for which there is considerable empirical evidence. However, I have decided to call them "hypotheses" rather than "findings" because the evidence is not sufficient—i.e., not yet available from a broad enough range of circumstances—to prove them in the abstract form in which I prefer to state them. Finally, there are a few conjectures I wish to assert without any systematic evidence.

Notation

The power of the model is derived largely from the highly abstract manner in which beliefs are represented. Each belief is represented as a function from a set of variables into a single variable. The first coordinating definition of a belief is the expectation of a person about how a set of causal factors have an effect on another factor. As the model progresses through its phases, additional interpretations are introduced for the same mathematical object. Some beliefs can also be interpreted as explanations, concepts, utility functions, and subjective probability distributions. The variables are just as abstract. They can be interpreted as observations, predicted values, payoffs, instruments, and several other things. Their values may be real numbers, but they do not have to be: they can also take on ordinal or even nominal values.

The notation for specific objects in the mathematical model will be introduced when the objects first appear in the model. However, to help the reader it might be useful to give a few of the symbols most often used. Variables are represented by the letter v with some one or more subscripts. A typical variable is represented as v_j. If two variables are needed, a prime is put on the subscript, so that the second variable will be called $v_{j'}$. In the second phase of the model, cases are introduced, and the subscript used for cases is i. Thus the value of the jth variable in the ith case is written v_{ij}. Beliefs are represented by the letter b with a subscript. A typical belief is represented as b_k. Each belief is a function from a set of variables into a single variable. The vector representing a typical set of variables in the range of b_k is denoted by a_k, and the variable which comprises the domain of b_k is denoted by v_k. To prevent the notation from getting unduly complicated, the same symbol is used for both the name of a variable or belief and the particular value that it may take on in a given situation.

Standard set theoretic notation is used throughout. For example, I is the set of all cases (i.e., the population), and iϵI means that i is a member of the set I. I'$\subset$I means that I' is a subset of I, and may equal I. A set of objects is denoted by braces, as in the set of all variables, $\{v_j\}_{j\epsilon J}$. An element in the Cartesian product of a family of sets is the vector consisting of one member from each set, and is denoted by an oversized X. For example, if J' is the index set of the variables in the range of belief b_k, then

$$a_k \in \underset{j\epsilon J'}{\bigtimes} v_j$$

Good old real numbers are symbolized by R. Summation over a set of real numbers is denoted by the familiar capital sigma, as in

$$\sum_{j\epsilon J'} v_j$$

where $v_j \epsilon R$ for each jϵJ'.

PHASE 1: THE BELIEVER

The Belief System

The first phase of the mathematical model describes a person who has a collection of beliefs about some variables. He does not yet have any data to support these beliefs, but the beliefs and variables themselves are enough raw material to start a mathematical model.

There are two primitives in the model for the believer:

Primitive 1:   A set V of elements called <u>variables</u>.

Primitive 2:   A set B of elements called <u>beliefs</u>.

The model of the believer also has two axioms:

Axiom 1:   V is finite and not empty.

Axiom 2:   B is finite, and each member of B is a function from the Cartesian product of some of the members of V into one of the members of V.

For convenience the set of variables will be labeled with a subscript, j. The index set of subscripts for the variables can thus be represented as J. A particular member of V, which is to say a particular variable, will be written v_j. This gives $V = \{v_j\}_{j \in J}$.

According to the second axiom, the beliefs can be regarded as functions. With the label k for beliefs we have for $b_k \in B$:

$$b_k: \bigtimes_{j' \in J'} v_{j'} \longrightarrow v_j \quad \text{for some } J' \subseteq J, \; j \in J.$$

The coordinating definitions of beliefs and variables point to something in the empirical world that the reader might want to think about when he sees one of the formal terms. A belief can be thought of as a cause-effect belief about how a particular set of variables affect (or determine, or cause) a single variable. A belief or set of beliefs can also be thought of as an explanation for a variable in terms of a set of variables. Later, several other interpretations will be given for particular systems of beliefs, but the two interpretations given here remain the basic ones. The variables can be thought of as the things about which the person has beliefs.

To determine the magnitude of expected change in a given variable, the effects transmitted by the entire set of beliefs which have that variable at their head are both necessary and sufficient. The effect transmitted by a single belief is sufficient but not necessary to produce an expected change in the variable at the head of its arrow.

5

Together the two primitives and the two axioms listed above make a mathematical object which can be called a belief system. The notation is that (V,B) is a belief system. When there is no doubt about which set of variables are being used, one can simply say that B is a belief system. The term <u>cognitive map</u> is used as a synonym for belief system when special emphasis is placed upon the structure of the set of beliefs.

It is handy to be able to draw a picture of a belief system. For this purpose variables can be represented as points. A belief can be represented as an arrow with several tails and one head. Figure 1 shows the picture of a belief, b_7, that v_1 and v_2 cause v_3. (In equation notation this is $b_7 (v_1, v_2) = v_3$.)

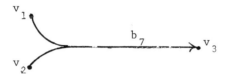

Figure 1. A Picture of a Belief

It is also handy to have a way to refer to the <u>tails and head of a belief</u>. Therefore, two functions will be defined for this purpose.

<u>Definition</u>: For b_k: $\underset{j' \varepsilon J'}{\bigwedge} v_{j'} \longrightarrow v_j$ for $J' \subset J$, $j \varepsilon J$

let $T(b_k) = J'$ and $H(b_k) = j$.

This means that T identifies the variables which are at the tail of the belief (i.e., the causes) and H identifies the variable which is at the head of the belief (i.e., the effect). In the example of Figure 1, $T(b_7) = \{1,2\}$ and $H(b_7) = 3$.

Note that nothing has been said about what specific values the variables may take. A particular variable may take on the values of specific numbers while another variable may take on values of a set of nominal categories. Therefore a belief system can handle any type of variable.

Since nothing has been said about what types of functions are allowed to be beliefs, a belief system also can include any type of function so long as it maps a set of variables into a specific variable. This allows for the possibility of interaction between the tail variables. It also means that a set of beliefs can be either consistent or inconsistent. Finally, beliefs may have more than one variable in their tail, but they may have just one. We now turn to the situation in which each belief has only one variable as a cause.

Nets

Simple Beliefs

All beliefs have one element in their head. Those beliefs which also have only one element in their tail can be called simple beliefs. We now formally define the set of simple beliefs.

Definition: $S = \{b_k \varepsilon B \mid T(b_k) = \{j'\}$ for some $j' \varepsilon J\}$

This suggests the definition of a simple cognitive system as a cognitive system in which all beliefs are simple.

Definition: (V, B_s) is a simple belief system if $B_s \subset S$.

The next step is to show that a simple cognitive system has the same structure as an abstract mathematical object called a net. This will allow the application of all the known properties of a net to any simple cognitive system.

Definition: A net (or a network) is a mathematical object with four primitives and two axioms. The primitives are V, X, f, s where f: X → V and s: X → V. The axioms are that V is finite and not empty and that X is finite (Harary et al., 1965, 5).

Theorem: A simple belief system is a net.

Proof: The proof is almost trivial. Let (V, B_s) be a simple belief system. Then the V of the cognitive system can serve as the V of the net, and the B_s can serve as the X. For $x = b_k \varepsilon X$, let $f(k) = v_j$, where $\{j'\} = T(b_k)$. This is possible because b_k is a simple belief with only one element in its tail. Likewise, for $x = b_k \varepsilon X$, let $s(x) = v_j$ where $j = H(b_k)$.

Digraphs

A specific type of net which is commonly used in the social sciences is a directed graph, or digraph for short. In pictorial terms a digraph is a net which has no loops or parallel lines. A loop is a simple arrow whose head is the same variable as its tail. Two lines (beliefs) are parallel if one has the same head and the same tail as the other.

The pictorial representation of a digraph is quite useful. Since all the beliefs are simple and there are no loops, each arrow goes from one (and only one) variable to some other variable. Since there are no parallel lines, no two arrows start and end in the same place. Under the coordinating definitions which have been suggested for a belief system, a digraph can be thought of as a set of single cause, single effect beliefs such that (1) no belief says that something causes itself directly and

7

(2) if two beliefs are about the same way one variable affects another, then they are the same belief.

All simple belief systems are nets, but they are not necessarily digraphs. The reader is referred to Harary et al. (1965) for an excellent treatment of digraphs. For now there is no need to require the added assumptions of digraphs, and the discussion can return to simple belief systems.

Logics on Simple Belief Systems

Under certain circumstances a person can derive a new belief by combining two old beliefs according to fixed rules. There are two basic situations in which combinations are appropriate. One is when the person has two beliefs about two different ways in which one variable affects another. The operation of combining these two parallel beliefs into a composite belief will be called addition. Addition of two beliefs is illustrated in Figure 2.

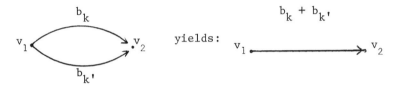

Figure 2. Addition of Two Beliefs

The second basic situation is when two beliefs occur in series. The tail of the second belief is the same variable as the head of the first. The operation of combining these two beliefs into one composite belief with the same tail as the first and the same head as the second is called multiplication. Multiplication of two beliefs is illustrated in Figure 3.

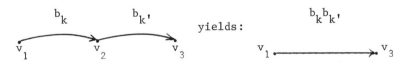

Figure 3. Multiplication of Two Beliefs

The first step in analyzing the various rules which can govern these operations is to give a name to an abstract set of rules.

Definition: A logic on a simple belief system is a pair of operations, addition and multiplication, such that

$$(b_k + b_{k'})(v_j) = b_k(v_j) + b_{k'}(v_j)$$

and

$$(b_{k} \cdot b_{k'})(v_{j}) = b_{k'}(b_{k}(v_{j})).$$

Note that in order for a simple belief system to have a logic it must have the operation of addition within its variables already defined. Once this is done, addition and multiplication can be defined for its beliefs. The first part of the definition of a logic simply says that the head of a belief derived from adding two beliefs is the sum of the heads of those two beliefs. The second part says that the product of two beliefs is simply the functional composition of the two beliefs.

The next step is to consider specific examples of logics. The first two will be called linear logic and binary logic. They can be regarded as normatively valid systems of deduction. The third example is psycho-logic, an invention of Abelson and Rosenberg (1958) meant to illustrate a system of deduction which people may actually use even though its deductions would (as the authors note) mortify a logician.

1. Linear Logic

Linear logic uses everyday arithmetic on variables which are all real numbers. The beliefs of a belief system with a linear logic are all linear, meaning that one variable is believed to be the linear combination of others.

Definition: A linear logic is the logic on a simple belief system which has $v_{j} \varepsilon R$ with arithmetic addition and multiplication, and $b_{k}(v_{j}) = r_{k}v_{j}$ for $r_{k} \varepsilon R$. This gives

$$(b_{k} + b_{k'}) = r_{k}v_{j} + r_{k'}v_{j}$$

and

$$(b_{k}b_{k'})(v_{j}) = r_{k'}r_{k}v_{j}$$

In linear logic, addition and multiplication of beliefs are associative and commutative because the corresponding operations on the variables are associative and commutative. The unit of addition is $b_{0}(v_{j}) = 0$, while the unit of multiplication is $b_{1}(v_{j}) = v_{j}$, and $b_{0} \neq b_{1}$.

Addition has an inverse given by $- b_{k}(v_{j}) = - r_{k}v_{j}$. Multiplication also has an inverse for all but $r_{k} = 0$, given by $b_{k}^{-1}(v_{j}) = v_{j}/r_{k}$. Finally, multiplication is distributive with respect to addition, $b_1 (b_2 + b_3) = b_1 b_2 + b_1 b_3$. Since these conditions are exactly those of a $\underline{field}$, the following theorem has been proved.

Theorem: The beliefs of a simple belief system with the operations of a linear logic comprise a field.

The reader may recognize linear logic as the set of rules used in the statistical discipline of causal inference (e.g., Blalock, 1961). It is also the set of rules used in circuit theory to handle signal flow diagrams (Busacker and Saaty, 1965).

It appears that researchers working in the three domains of cognitive processes, causal inference, and circuit theory are ignorant of each other's work. The only exception seems to be Stinchcombe (1968), who makes one of the associations--namely the one between causal inference and circuit theory. But he treats causality as a set of formal concepts and does not use the statistical literature of Blalock and others. The explanation for the independence of these three fields probably lies in their very different intellectual roots. The work on cognitive processes has been done mainly by psychologists, that on causal inference by statisticians and econometricians, and that on circuit theory by physical scientists and mathematicians.

An immediate gain from using the research in these other areas is that they provide a set of ready-made formal tools. For example, circuit theorists have discovered a solution to a problem which can appear in a formally equivalent form in belief systems. The problem is how to handle a belief whose head is the same variable as its tail--i.e., a loop.

Theorem: In linear logic a loop with an operator q can be replaced by a new belief from the original one to a dummy variable, where the new belief has an

operator $\dfrac{1}{1-q}$.

This theorem asserts that the two diagrams of Figures 4 and 5 are equivalent in linear logic. A brief discussion of this principle is given in Stinchcombe (1968, 133-38), and a demonstration of the proof is given in Busaker and Saaty (1965, 186-92).

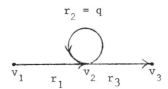

$r_2 = q$

$v_1 \quad r_1 \quad v_2 \quad r_3 \quad v_3$

Figure 4. Net with a Loop

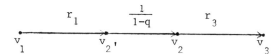

Figure 5. Equivalent Net without a Loop

2. Binary Logic

The second example of a logic on a belief system employs variables which can take on only two values, such as 0 and 1, or False and True. The operations on the variables will be those of symbolic logic. To be concrete, the Hilbert-Ackerman propositional calculus whose basic operations on the variables are negation and weak (i.e., inclusive) disjunction symbolized by - and v respectively (Copi, 1954, 239). In binary logic addition can be identified with disjunction ("or"), while multiplication can be identified with conjunction ("and").

Definition: A **binary logic** is the logic on a simple belief system which has $v_j \varepsilon \{0,1\}$ and Hilbert-Ackerman operations on v_j. This gives

$$b_k \cdot b_{k'}(v_j) = b_{k'}(b_k(v_j))$$

and

$$(b_k + b_{k'})(v_j) = b_k(v_j) \text{ v } b_{k'}(v_j)$$

The Hilbert-Ackerman logic is functionally complete, which means that all truth functions can be expressed in terms of "compound" statements compounded using only the basic operations (in this case - and v). For example, multiplication (conjunction) can be expressed as

$$b_k \cdot b_{k'} = -(-b_k \text{ v } - b_{k'}).$$

Binary logic is associative and commutative. Addition and multiplication are distributive both ways. The unit of addition is 0, while the unit of multiplication is 1. There is no additive inverse for 1 and no multiplicative inverse for 0.

The coordinating definition of binary logic is the familiar two-valued deductive logic of Aristotle. Thus just as linear logic can be thought of as a normatively valid set of rules for combining beliefs about variables that take on numerical values, binary logic can be thought of as a normatively valid set of rules for combining beliefs about variables that take on only the values of True or False.

3. Psycho-logic

Psycho-logic is a mathematical system invented by Abelson and Rosenberg (1958) to demonstrate how people actually deduce new attitudes--as opposed to the way they ought to. The system is internally consistent. What makes it invalid from a normative point of view is the coordinating definitions attached to the values that the beliefs may take on.

In psycho-logic there are four types of beliefs, labelled p, n, a, and 0. Thus $K = \{p,n,a,0\}$. The terms can be read as "positive," "negative," "ambivalent," and "null" respectively. They can be thought of as attitudes loaded with affect or as causal beliefs.* Thus, using Abelson and Rosenberg's coordinating definition, $v_2 = b_p(v_1)$ can mean that v_1 likes, supports, uses, advocates, helps, promotes, brings about, serves, justifies, or is consistent with v_2. Using a more restricted coordinating definition the same equation would be taken to mean that v_1 causes, promotes, or brings about v_2. The negative relationship, n, stands for dislikes or hinders. With a strict causal interpretation, $v_2 = b_n(v_1)$ might mean that _ceteris paribus_ the more v_1 there is, the less v_2 there is. The null relation, 0, stands for indifference or unrelatedness. Peitzer (1969) recommends "may or may not lead to" as a better coordinating definition of 0. The ambivalent relation, a, holds when there is a conjunction of positive and negative relations.

Abelson and Rosenberg (1958) define a set of rules for addition and multiplication of these terms. However, there has been some confusion about exactly what these rules mean in formal terms (Lambert, 1966; Giese, 1967), but now it seems nicely worked out (Peitzer, 1969). I will follow Peitzer's interpretation, and use the symbol to render Abelson and Rosenberg's null relation as interpreted by Peitzer's j. The formal definition of psycho-logic is given in the next definition.

Definition: A psycho-logic is the logic on a simple belief system which has $K = \{p,n,a,0\}$ and operations defined by:

    (1) $k + 0 = k$
    (2) $k + k = k$
    (3) $k + a = a$
    (4) $p + n = a$
    (5) $k \cdot p = k$
    (6) $k \cdot 0 = 0$
    (7) $k \cdot a = a$ for $k \neq 0$

---

*Abelson and Rosenberg even allow the variables to represent actors, but this possibility will not be considered here.

PHASE 1: THE BELIEVER

$$(8) \quad n \cdot n = p$$
$$(9) \quad k + k' = k' + k$$
$$(10) \quad k \cdot k' = k' \cdot k$$

In these rules k and k' are any element of K. In the notation of simple belief systems the first rule says

$$v_2 = b_k(v_1) \text{ and } v = b_0(v_1) \text{ implies } v_2 = b_k(v_1).$$

For example, with k = n, this rule says that if there are a negative belief and a null belief about the relationship between two variables, the beliefs can be added together to give a negative belief.

The eighth rule deals with multiplication:

$$v_2 = b_n(v_1) \text{ and } v_3 = b_n(v_2) \text{ implies } v_3 = b_p(v_1).$$

This means that if v_1 is believed to hinder v_2 and v_2 is believed to hinder v_3, then v_1 is believed to help v_3.

The ninth and tenth rules assert symmetry for addition and multiplication.

The effect of the rules can be presented in the addition and multiplication tables given below.

Table 1

ADDITION TABLE FOR BELIEFS IN PSYCHO-LOGIC

+	p	n	0	a
p	p	a	p	a
n	a	n	n	a
0	p	n	0	a
a	a	a	a	a

Table 2

MULTIPLICATION TABLE FOR BELIEFS IN PSYCHO-LOGIC

.	p	n	0	a
p	p	n	0	a
n	n	p	0	a
0	0	0	0	0
a	a	a	0	a

13

To illustrate how psycho-logic can lead to "illogical" conclusions, here is an example from Abelson and Rosenberg (1958, 4-5):

India opposes U.S. Far Eastern policy.
U.S. Far Eastern policy is directed against Communism.
Therefore, India is in favor (p) of Communism.

The authors comment that "Such 'reasoning' would mortify a logician, yet it can be found in much this form inside millions of heads."

A similar example is given next. Now only cause-effect beliefs are used, instead of affect relations, and the notation of simple belief systems is employed.

Indian effort (v_1) is directed against (n) the effectiveness of U.S. Far Eastern policy (v_2).
The effectiveness of U.S. Far Eastern policy (v_2) weakens (n) the strength of Communism (v_3).
Therefore, Indian effort (v_1) promotes (p) Communist strength (v_3).

The reasoning is:

$$v_2 = b_n(v_1)$$
$$v_3 = b_n(v_2)$$

Therefore (by rule 8) $v_3 = b_p(v_1)$.

One way to regard the mistake in both examples is the categorization of different objects into the same term. In actuality India does not oppose all aspects of U.S. Far Eastern policy, and not all aspects of U.S. Far Eastern policy fight Communism. Thus, the mistaken conclusion is based upon an over-generalization of terms by the believer, rather than a mistake in calculation. The process of generalizing and categorizing is called concept formation, and it can be formally studied in the context of belief systems, as will be seen later.

This section on logic has considered how a person might combine old beliefs to derive new beliefs. Another question is how a person might decide to change a few of his beliefs to bring them into line with all the rest of his beliefs. We now look at a major empirical theory designed to answer that question--namely, the theory of cognitive consistency.

Cognitive Consistency and Balance

The theory of cognitive consistency starts with the notion of a balanced belief system. The coordinating definition of balance is that all variables are either "black" or "white," and

14

all beliefs are consistent with these groupings. In a balanced belief system there are no ambivalent beliefs, and it is impossible to derive an ambivalent belief from the others.

> Definition: A simple belief system is balanced if the set of variables can be partitioned into two sets (one of which may be empty) such that all the beliefs between variables in the same set are positive or null, and all the beliefs between variables in different sets are negative or null.*

The idea that a person tries to achieve balance in his belief system has been hypothesized by Heider (1946), Osgood and Tannenbaum (1955), Festinger (1957), and others. A way to state this hypothesis in formal terms was independently discovered by Abelson and Rosenberg (1958) and Harary (in Harary et al., 1965).

The procedure is to first define the amount of imbalance in a set of simple beliefs and then to specify the easiest way to remove the imbalance by changing the fewest number of beliefs. As before, the simple beliefs can be pictured as lines connecting variables which are pictured as points.

> Definition: The line index of a simple belief system is the least number of beliefs that must be negated to get a balanced set of beliefs. Such a set of lines is called an alternation-minimal set.

The hypothesis about how people actually change their beliefs (or attitudes) to resolve imbalance is stated by Harary et al. (1965, 351f) in the form of an "if . . . then" proposition which is here translated into the language of belief systems.

> Line Index Hypothesis: If the principle of "least cost" governs balancing processes, and the change of each belief requires the same cost, then the beliefs of an alternation-minimal set will be susceptible to change and the line index is a measure of the cost required to attain balance.

The assumptions required to make the line index hypothesis valid are rather powerful, and are almost certainly not strictly valid. A more accurate hypothesis would take into account the

---

*Harary et al. (1965, 342) give this definition as a theorem derived from an equivalent definition of balance. I am generalizing both Harary et al. and Abelson and Rosenberg from digraphs to nets.

strength with which each belief is held. Nevertheless, in cases where it takes about as much "effort" to change one belief as it does another, the hypothesis may be a fair approximation.

The line index hypothesis incorporates one of the main ideas of the literature of cognitive consistency. That idea is that individuals strive toward consistent (or balanced) cognitions and tend to attain consistency in the "easiest" possible way. Yet the line index hypothesis is undoubtedly too simple to be accurate. In particular it ignores the possibility that the beliefs represented by some lines may be much less susceptible to change than the beliefs represented by other lines.

Some interesting relationships between binary logic and psycho-logic are provided by the next two theorems.

Theorem: Binary logic is isomorphic to psycho-logic when there are no ambivalent or negative beliefs.

Proof: The relevant portions of the addition and multiplication tables of psycho-logic are equivalent to the truth tables of disjunction and conjunction respectively.

Theorem: Every set of beliefs in binary logic is balanced.

Proof: All the variables can be put in one set with positive or null relations between them.

Concept Formation

Much as a logic is a method of deriving new beliefs by combining old ones, concept formation is a method of deriving new variables by combining old ones. Concepts are extremely important because they provide the categories a person uses to think. The results of his thinking will be heavily influenced by the categories he uses.

By treating the process of concept formation in a formal way, the variables themselves can be thought of as the dimensions (or attributes) that are relevant to a specifying concept. This suggests that the variables themselves can be the result of the process of concept formation--and indeed they can. However, for analytical purposes this potentially infinite regress must stop somewhere with a set of variables that are given a priori. Then concept formation can be done on these variables to derive new variables, and concepts can be formed with the new variables, and so on indefinitely in that direction.

PHASE 1: THE BELIEVER

Informally, a concept is a method of categorization. There are two extra properties that concepts are usually assumed to have and which can be added to the definition (Garner, 1962, 310-312). One is that there are fewer categories than there were original objects. Otherwise the categorization is trivial. Second, there must be more than one dimension (or attribute) which is used in the categorization process. Otherwise the process is merely a collapsing of the values on one dimension into fewer values, rather than the formation of a new concept. The formal definition follows.

> Definition: A concept is a many-to-one belief which is not simple.

The formal definition is very cogent, but it requires some explanation. It says that a concept is a type of belief. Recall that a belief is a function from a set of variables into a single variable. This is how a concept can define a new variable based upon several old variables. The new variable is simply the head of the concept.

The definition of a many-to-one function is a familiar one in algebra.

> Definition: A function, f, is many-to-one if there exist two objects in the range of f, a, and b, such that a $\neq$ b and such that f(a) = f(b).

A belief that is not simple must by the definition of a simple belief have more than one variable in its tail. These variables can be thought of as the dimensions or attributes which the concept employs. Therefore a many-to-one non-simple belief satisfies the two informal conditions for a concept: it is a non-trivial categorization and it involves more than one dimension or attribute. Note that since a concept is not a simple belief, it cannot appear in a net. Therefore, the material presented earlier on logics and cognitive consistency does not apply to concepts.

Of course a belief which is interpreted as a concept can also be thought of as a cause-effect belief merely by saying that the head variable is caused (or determined) by the set of tail variables. The interesting questions are how a person comes to employ one concept rather than another and what difference it makes. These questions will be postponed until the notions of data and accuracy are introduced. The same questions can be dealt with in even more adequate form when the additional notions from information theory and decision-making are presented.

17

PHASE 2: THE OBSERVER

Data

The first phase of the model deals only with a person in his role as believer. He has beliefs, but no data to form and reform them. The second phase of the model introduces data and examines some of the implications a body of data has for single beliefs and for sets of beliefs.

For our purposes, data are defined as the observations a person makes (Coombs, 1964). These observations are assumed to be coded in terms of specific values of the variables in the person's belief system. There is an easy way to formalize this conception of data without introducing any new primitive terms.

Definition: Let $v_j = \{v_{ij}\}_{i \in I}$; then $D_{I'J'} = \{v_{ij}\}_{i \in I'}$, $j \in J'$

where $I' \subset I$ and $J' \subset J$.

This means that each variable, v_j, is defined as a vector over the index i. The index i can be thought of as representing a <u>case</u>. The first part of the definition then means that each variable is a set of observations, one for each case. If i and j are integers, then the set of all possible observations can be represented as a large matrix V_{IJ} with entries v_{ij} for case i and variable j.

The data themselves can be regarded as a subset of all possible observations. The appropriate subset is the one restricted to only some of the cases, $I' \subset I$, and some of the variables, $J' \subset J$. The set of cases in which there are data is the <u>sample</u>, I'. The set of variables for which there are data can be thought of as the <u>observed variables</u>, J'. All of this can be represented in matrix form, as in Figure 6. In this figure the data have been moved to a corner of the matrix by permutations of the indices.

A case can be thought of in the usual statistical sense. If observations are being made about the gross national product, a case might correspond to a time unit, such as a year. If observations are being made about wars, a case might be an episode such as World War II. If observations are being made about public opinion, a case might be the opinion of a single person (who is typically not the person making the observations). The set of all possible cases is the <u>population</u>. The particular sample upon which the actual observations are being made is a subset of the population. There is no need to assume any restrictions on the size of the population, although the sample is usually thought of as being finite in size.

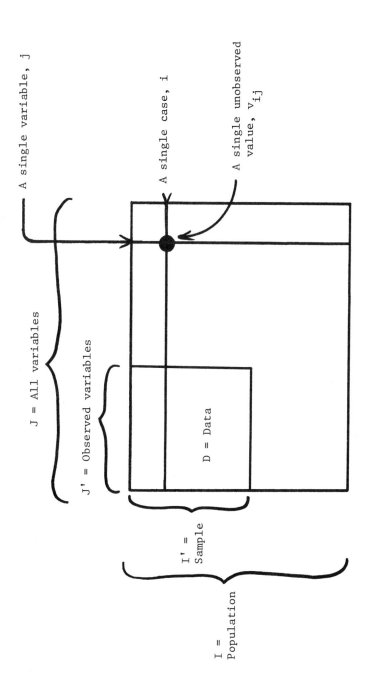

Figure 6.   The Matrix V of Cases by Variables

Now that the notion of data has been introduced, the accuracy of a belief can be considered. However, before the discussion becomes too complex, it will help to introduce some streamlined notation.

Definitions: $j_k = H(b_k)$ (1)

$$v_{ik} = v_{ij_k}$$ (2)

$$v_k = v_{j_k}$$ (3)

$$a_k \in \bigtimes_{j \varepsilon T(b_k)} v_j$$ (4)

$$a_{ik} \in \bigtimes_{j \varepsilon T(b_k)} v_{ij}$$ (5)

The first definition provides a convenient way to refer to the variable which is at the head (or range) of a particular belief. The second definition specifies a way to refer to the value of the variable in a given case. The third definition shows how the value of a belief can be represented as the value of the variable corresponding to that belief. The fourth definition indicates a general element in the domain of a belief by selecting a single value for each of the variables in the tail of the belief. The last definition specifies the element in the tail (or domain) of the belief that corresponds to a particular case. Of course an element in the tail of a belief is--in general--a vector, and can be regarded as a part of some case.

Accuracy of a Belief

Types of Accuracy

A set of beliefs can be thought of as accurate if it gives the right answer using specific values of the variables. The right answer is defined in terms of the observed value of the variable at the head of the belief. The "accuracy" of the observation itself is beyond the scope of the present model of belief systems. A person can check only the accuracy of his beliefs, and he must take his observations for granted. This is not as restrictive as it may seem, because the meaning of an observation can change when the beliefs about that variable change.

Definition: A set of beliefs, $\{b_k\}$, is accurate with respect to a sample if $\sum_k b_k(a_{ik}) = v_{ik}$ for all cases

in the sample, where the summation is taken
over the index of the set of beliefs.

Similar definitions can be given for accuracy with respect
to a single case and with respect to the entire population. An
explanation of a set of variables is formed by a set of beliefs
which together give an accurate account of each variable in the
set. Like accuracy, explanation can be defined with respect to
a single case, a sample, or the entire population.

A deduction is a result derived under the assumption that
the relevant beliefs are accurate. Thus the process of deduction
allows a believer to calculate the expected consequences of
changes in the values of the variables at the tails of his beliefs. It also allows him to reason backwards from effects to
causes by using the inverse of particular beliefs. One of the
main uses of deduction for the observer is to derive an estimate
of an unobserved variable based upon the values of some observed
variables and the beliefs which link them.

S-R Learning

Stimulus-response learning can be interpreted in terms
of belief systems. The stimulus is a_{ik}. This is a set of values
on one or more dimensions for a particular case. The relevant
part of the organism is his (or its) means of translating the
stimulus into the response. This translation method can be
thought of as a single function, b_k. This makes $b_k(a_{ik})$ the
response to the stimulus. A particular response is accurate (or
more properly, a particular b_k is accurate) if $b_k(a_{ik}) = v_{ik}$. A
typical stimulus-response learning problem presents the partial
cases in a sample of data in sequential form as the stimuli (a_{ik})
and asks for a sequence of responses, $(b_k(a_{ik}))$. If the beliefs
are sufficiently close to being accurate, learning is said to
take place. To measure closeness to accuracy there must be a
metric on the response variable, j_k, and this metric defines the
performance criteria. Concept learning is the special case in
which an accurate belief is a concept. In discrimination and ab-
solute judgment tasks, accuracy might require only a simple belief.

Relation to Balance

A set of beliefs with psycho-logic may be balanced without being accurate. Suppose, for example, that the only belief
linking v_1 and v_2 is $b_p(v_1) = v_2$. Now suppose that in case i the
person observes $v_{i1} = p$ and $v_{i2} = n$. This makes the belief inac-
curate for that case. Thus a belief in a balanced set might not
be accurate. This also means that a balanced set of beliefs
might not be an explanation of a given case.

FRAMEWORK FOR A GENERAL THEORY OF COGNITION AND CHOICE

Information Transmission of a Belief

Uncertainty

The application of information theory to problems of cognition has been very fruitful. Garner (1962) provides an excellent account. In this paper it will suffice to show how information theory can be handled in terms of belief systems, and to give a few examples of some of the more important and better-tested hypotheses. What follows is largely a translation of Garner into language compatible with belief systems.

Information reduces ignorance or uncertainty about the state of things. The state of things can be thought of as the specific values that the variables take on over a range of cases. The amount of information is determined by the amount by which uncertainty is reduced. It is a function of the number of things which could have happened but did not.

First, let us define probability. Consider a sample I', and a variable v_{ij} which takes on different values in different cases--say q_1, q_2, q_3, etc. The probability that the variable will take on a specific value is the number of cases in which it has that value divided by the total number of cases. This defines $p(v_{ij} = q)$ as a __probability distribution__ of variable j over sample I'.

Definition:
$$p(v_j = q) = \frac{\text{size } \{v_{ij} \mid v_{ij} = q\}_{i \in I'}}{\text{size } \{i\}_{i \in I'}}$$

Thus p is a function from a value q into the real numbers between 0 and 1. When thinking of the entire distribution over all cases in the sample (or the population), and for all values of q, it is sufficient to write $p(v_j)$ for the probability distribution of variable j.

The fundamental notion in information theory is the __average uncertainty__ of a variable. The average uncertainty, $U(v_j)$, is defined in terms of the probability distribution, $p(v_j)$.

Definition: $U(v_j) = - \sum_q p(v_j = q) \log_2 p(v_j = q)$.

When the sample and the set of values of v_j are understood, this formula can be written $U(v_j) = - \Sigma \, p(v_j) \log p(v_j)$. In information theory the base of the logarithm is taken to be 2 for convenience.

In learning experiments, the variable can be thought of as the stimulus, v_s, or as the correct response, v_r. Then $U(v_s)$

is <u>stimulus uncertainty</u>, and $U(v_r)$ is <u>response uncertainty</u>. When the task is accurately learned, $v_r = b_k(v_s)$. After reviewing a number of experiments, Garner (1962, 52) formulates two well-established hypotheses that are of interest here.

<u>Hypothesis</u>: Learning is more difficult if either $U(v_s)$ or $U(v_r)$ is increased.

<u>Hypothesis</u>: Perceptual discrimination, measured by number of errors of identification, becomes better if $U(v_s)$ is reduced by reducing the size of $\{q_s\}$.

Note that so far nothing has been said about restrictions on the variable, v_j, except that it has a probability distribution over its range of values $\{q_j\}$. This allows the interpretation of the definition of uncertainty to be extended to apply to multi-dimensional values. For example, <u>joint uncertainty</u> of two variables can be defined as

$$U(v_j, v_{j'}) = - \Sigma \, p(v_j, v_{j'}) \, \log p(v_j, v_{j'})$$

where $p(v_j, v_{j'})$ is the joint probability. The maximum joint uncertainty given the uncertainty of v_j and $v_{j'}$, occurs when v_j and $v_{j'}$ are independent. Independence means

$$p(v_j, v_{j'}) = p(v_j) \, p(v_{j'})$$

Using the shorthand of letting j stand for v_j, the definition of <u>maximum uncertainty</u> can be expressed as follows:

Definition: $U_{max}(j, j') = U(j, j')$ for $p(j, j') = p(j) \, p(j')$.

The following theorem follows from these definitions with a little algebraic manipulation:

<u>Theorem</u>: $U_{max}(j, j') = U(j) + U(j')$.

The next key definition is for <u>contingent uncertainty</u>. This is the reduction in joint uncertainty due to the correlation of v_j and $v_{j'}$.

<u>Definition</u>: $U(j: j') = U_{max}(j, j') - U(j, j')$

For the purposes of studying cognition, the most useful interpretation of contingent uncertainty is a measure of information transfer through a communication system. The set of stimuli, v_{is} (or a_{is} if a stimulus is multi-dimensional), can be considered as the input to the person, and the person's response, $b_k(a_{is})$, can be thought of as the output of the system. The person himself is the communication system. The contingent uncertainty between the input and the output $(U(a_s: b_k(a_s))$ is the amount of <u>information transmission</u> of a belief in a given sample.

Channel Capacity

Many communication systems have an upper bound on the amount of information they can transfer. If the input (or stimulus) has less uncertainty than this limit, all of the information can be transferred to the output (or response). However, if the input has more uncertainty than the channel can handle, the communication system transfers only as much as it can.

Definition: C is a <u>channel capacity</u> of a communication system if

$$U(a_s: b_k(a_s)) = U(v_s) \text{ for } U(v_s) \leq C$$

$$U(a_s: b_k(a_s)) = C \text{ for } U(v_s) > C$$

This definition is illustrated in Figure 7.

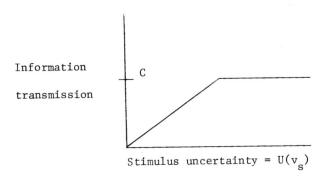

Figure 7. Channel Capacity

The point of all this can be made by listing a series of well-established hypotheses about channel capacity; they are paraphrased and translated from Garner (1962).

Hypothesis: Humans have a channel capacity for perceptual discrimination.

This hypothesis asserts that there is an upper bound to the ability of a person to discriminate between stimuli. The functions, $\{b_k\}$, can be thought of as perceptual discrimination because they relate stimuli to responses. Thus the channel capacity hypothesis can probably be interpreted as the assertion of a limit upon the "sophistication" (or "complexity") of any belief that a person can hold without resorting to external aids.

How far the channel capacity hypothesis can be generalized and applied beyond the domain of perceptual discrimination experiments remains to be seen. Assuming that the hypothesis is indeed well-established for one kind of experiment (as it is), and assuming that it refers to a basic property of human cognition (as it seems to), the range of valid application is likely to be quite broad.

Not only is a channel capacity known to exist, but a number of things are known about its size.

Hypothesis: For most uni-dimensional perceptual continua, the channel capacity is quite stable and low, having a value of about 2.3 bits.

The number 2.3 bits is approximately equivalent to five equally likely categories. Although the magnitude is open to some measurement error and varies some from one type of experiment to another, the same idea was advanced in Miller's classic article (1956), "The Magic Number Seven, Plus or Minus Two."

Hypothesis: The channel capacity can be increased by the use of perceptual anchors (or fixed reference points).

Hypothesis: The channel capacity for perceptual discrimination can be increased by training the person over extended periods of time.

Hypothesis: The channel capacity is greater for multi-dimensional stimuli than for single dimensional stimuli. The information transferred is actually less per dimension, but the total information transmission is greater.

The next hypothesis is the conclusion of only one set of experiments (by Eriksen and Wechsler [1955]), but it is interesting enough to mention.

Hypothesis: Anxiety does not lower information transmission, although it does cause a stereotyping of response (i.e., it lowers response uncertainty).

Information theory has also been helpful in understanding the empirical process of concept learning, as the next two hypotheses show.

25

Hypothesis: Concept learning is most efficient (information transmission is maximized sooner) when the correct responses are assigned to the stimuli in such a manner as to minimize the number of relevant variables.

Hypothesis: Concept learning is more difficult when the stimuli presented are primarily negative instances (instances of what the concept is not).

This result was obtained by Bruner, Goodnow and Austin (1956) among others, but Hovland (1952) suggests that it may be due to the fact that more information is provided by the positive instances in the samples used.

Another useful idea in information theory is redundancy. However, this subject is too complex to treat briefly here. The interested reader is referred to Garner (1962), who provides an excellent discussion of redundancy in terms of structure and constraint.

One final observation on channel capacity will serve to illustrate another facet of its potential importance to the study of belief systems. The observation is that if the response uncertainty is greater than the channel capacity, then the belief cannot be accurate.

Theorem: For a given sample I', and any b_k such that $U(a_s: b_k(a_s)) \leq C$, it is true that $U(v_r) > C$ implies b_k is not I'-accurate.

Proof: $U(v_r) > C$ implies $U(v_r) > U(a_s: b_k(a_s))$ by $C \geq U(a_s: b_k(a_s))$, which in turn is true by the definition of C. Now since $b_k(a_s)$ is a function of a_s, the conditional uncertainty of $b_k(a_s)$, given a_s, is zero.* Therefore $U(b_k(a_s)) = U(a_s: b_k(a_s))$. Thus $U(v_r) > C$ implies $U(v_r) > U(b_k(a_s))$, and this in turn implies that $v_r \neq b_k(a_s)$, which means that b_k is not accurate.

The significance of this theorem is that no belief which is limited by a channel capacity can accurately explain a variable which embodies too much information over a given sample. Thus, as long as a person's perceptual discrimination, b_k, is limited, there may be some variables which he cannot fully explain over an entire sample.

---

*The conditional uncertainty of y, given x, is $U_x(y) = U(y) - U(x:y)$. This is also the average uncertainty in y when x is held constant (see Garner, 1962, 57-59).

PHASE 3: THE PREDICTOR

Prediction Processes

The ability to construct new mathematical objects from old ones is an important property of a mathematical model. The construction of a new belief from two or more old beliefs has already been treated with the use of different types of logic. The construction of a new variable from one or more old variables has been treated with the use of beliefs such as concepts. The next topic is the construction of a new belief from one or more old variables.

Suppose a person observes a set of data. This means he observes the specific value taken on by each of a set of variables J', on each of a sample of cases, I'. This specifies the data matrix $D_{I'J'}$. Given this data, the person might ask himself how he can use some of the variables to explain the other variables. For example, he might want to explain just one of the variables in terms of all the others. This means that he will want to construct a belief whose tail and head are both in the set J'. The purpose of this construction might go beyond the question of how to explain a variable over the known sample, and might aim at being able to predict (more or less accurately) something about a brand new case.

To handle this operation of constructing a belief from a set of data, the introduction of a new primitive and a new axiom is in order.

Primitive 3: A set P of elements called prediction processes.

Axiom 3:   Each member of P is a function from a set of data into a belief whose head and tail are in the set of variables of the data.

With the label $l \epsilon L$ for prediction process, the notation for a particular process will be p_l. Then each prediction process, p_l, maps whole data sets into specific beliefs, as follows:

$$p_l: \quad D_{I'J'} \longrightarrow b_k \text{ where } T(b_k) \cup \{H(b_k)\} \subset J'$$

Thus p_l maps a matrix into a function, and the resulting function is a way of mapping a set of columns of the matrix into one of the columns of the matrix. The columns of the data matrix are, by definition, the observed variables.

Given a particular prediction process $p_l \epsilon P$, and a particular data set $D_{I'J'}$, one can determine a particular belief b_k such that

$$b_k: \quad a_k \longrightarrow v_k \qquad \text{where}$$

a_k is an element of the Cartesian product of some of the observed variables--i.e.,

$$a_k \underset{j \in J''}{} v_j$$

where $J'' \subset J'$ and where v_k is one of the observed variables. J'' is known as the set of <u>independent variables</u> of the prediction process, and the head of b_k is the <u>dependent variable</u>.

Given a data set $D_{I'J'}$, a prediction process p_1, and the independent variables of a particular case i, a_{ik}, one can construct a <u>prediction</u> for the specific value of the dependent variable. The method is easy. First, get b_k by $b_k = p_1(D_{I'J'})$, and then compute the value of the dependent variable as $b_k(a_{ik})$. Using the composition of the functions p_1 and b_k, this can be condensed into $(p_1(D_{I'J'}))(a_{ik})$.

The idea of accuracy can be extended to prediction processes. The method is to associate the accuracy of the process with the accuracy of the belief it gives on a particular sample, say I''.

Definition: p_1 is q-accurate when applied to a data set, $D_{I''J'}$, if $p_1(D_{I''J'})$ is q-accurate where q = {i, I', I}.

Regression

Two examples of a prediction process will help make the discussion more concrete. The first example is the familiar one of linear regression, where the variables are all real numbers.

To be more specific, let p_1 be the prediction process of least-squares linear regression of two independent variables, v_1 and v_2, on one dependent variable, v_3. Suppose there are twenty cases, each with a known value of all three variables, and suppose there is a twenty-first case in which only the independent variables are known. This example can be used to illustrate the notation of belief systems.

I' = the sample, composed of 20 cases

$J' = \{v_1, v_2, v_3\}$

$D_{I'J'}$ = a 20 x 3 matrix of observations

$H(b_k) = \{v_1, v_2\}$

28

$$T(b_k) = v_3$$

The linear regression will use the data to produce a function of the form

$$b_k(a_k) = b_0 + b_1 v_1 + b_2 v_2 \text{ where } a_k = (v_1, v_2)$$

The method used by regression is to select the coefficient in such a way as to minimize the sum of squares of the errors,

$$\sum_{i=1}^{20} (v_{i3} - b_k(v_{i1}, v_{i2}))^2$$

Now suppose that the values of the coefficients which minimize the error over the sample are $b_0 = 0$, $b_1 = 1$, and $b_2 = 3$. This means that $p_1(D_{I'J'}) = v_1 + 3v_2$. If the independent variables of the twenty-first case are $v_1 = 2$ and $v_2 = 5$, the prediction for the value of the dependent variable is

$$p_1(D_{I'J'})(a_{21_k}) = p_1(D_{I'J'})(2,5)$$

$$= 2 + 3 \text{ x } 5$$

$$= 17$$

If it happens that $v_{ij} = 17$ for $i = 21$ and $j = 3$, then p_1 is i-accurate (for case 21) when p_1 is applied to this particular data set (of 20 cases).

Returning to the more abstract level, regression can be specified in the same way as any prediction process can be specified--namely, by indicating which belief it will associate with any given set of data. The formal definition of <u>linear regression</u> follows:

Definition: For each $v_{ij} \varepsilon R$, $p_r \varepsilon P$ is defined by $p_r(D_{I'J'}) = b_k$

where $b_k(a_{ik}) = b_0 + \sum_{j \varepsilon J'} b_j v_{ij}$ such that $m(v_k, b_k(a_k))$ is minimized, where m is the Euclidean metric in the space of cases.

Linear regression can be (and usually is) thought of as a normative prediction process. It is normatively valid in the sense that it gives the best linear function through a set of data points, where "best" is defined as the least error on the dependent variable over the sample. The selected function is also "best" in the sense that it yields the "best" prediction for a new case, where "best" is defined statistically with certain assumptions about the randomness of error.

To use linear regression on an actual set of data requires a considerable amount of calculation. Even with thousands of cases and dozens of variables, this is easy for a computer. However, with more than a few cases and a very few variables, it becomes virtually impossible for a human being to do in his head, or even a human being aided by pencil and paper. However, people can closely approximate the linear function given by regression if there is only one independent variable, and if the data points are plotted on paper.

Incidentally, some types of nonlinear regression provide no real difficulty--for a computer. The method is to construct new independent variables from old variables with nonlinear beliefs. For example, a quadratic regression of v_1 on v_3 can be performed by using linear regression on $b_k(v_3) = b_0 + b_1 v_1 + b_2 v_2$ where $v_2 = b_k'(v_1) = v_1^2$.

Closest Point Estimation

The second example of a prediction process is much easier to compute than the first, but much less satisfactory from a normative point of view. For lack of a better name, I will call this prediction process "closest point estimation." The idea is to select the single case from the sample which most resembles the new case in terms of the values of the independent variables. Then the prediction of value of the dependent variable of the new case is simply the value of the dependent variable of the selected case. The formal definition of "closest point estimation" is:

Definition: $p_c \varepsilon P$ is defined by $p_c(D_{I'J'}) = b_k$ where $b_k(a_{ik}) = a_{i'k}$ for some $i' \varepsilon I'$ such that $m(a_{ik}, a_{i'k})$ is minimized, where m is a given metric in the space of independent variables.

If all of the variables are real numbers, the metric can be the familiar Euclidean distance between two points. In general a metric function is defined as follows:

Definition: m is a metric on a space Q if m: $Q \times Q \to R$ such that for a, b, $c \varepsilon Q$:

(1) $m(a,b) \geq 0$

(2) $m(a,b) = 0$ if and only if $a = b$

PHASE 3: THE PREDICTOR

$$(3) \quad m(a,b) = m(b,a)$$

$$(4) \quad m(a,b) + m(b,c) \geq m(a,c)$$

A person who uses closest point estimation has a much easier computational task than one who uses regression. In closest point estimation, when a person observes the independent variables of a new case, he merely has to scan the old cases to see which old case is closest to the new one. Then he predicts that the value of the dependent variable in the old case will be the same in the new case.

The problems with closest point estimation are threefold. First, it is inefficient from a statistical point of view because it fully employs only one case rather than the entire range of cases, as regression does. Second, it requires the user to remember the values of each of the variables in each of the cases, whereas regression requires him to remember only the coefficients that define the prediction belief. Finally, it requires a way to compare independent variables in determining the metric, whereas regression is essentially invariant with respect to the units of the independent variables.

Closest point estimation has an advantage over regression when:

(1) Computation is difficult;

(2) There are few cases; and

(3) There are many independent variables.

These conditions are typical of international relations. Individuals do not know how to use information-processing tools to aid their computation because they do not know how to code their information. There is usually very little relevant experience upon which to base one's predictions. (For example, the number of outbreaks of war in the lifetime of a diplomat is likely to be relatively small--fortunately.) Finally, the number of factors which potentially can contribute to the explanation of an important feature of international politics is likely to be quite large.

Whenever the conditions which give closest point estimation the advantage prevail, I conjecture that it (or a similar prediction process) will be employed. Since these conditions are often found in international relations, it seems likely that some such process will be used by people who are trying to explain or predict any of the various aspects of international relations. In support of this conjecture, I note that people often use historical analogies and often draw general lessons from specific cases in their analyses of international politics. The case of

31

Munich, for example, is still used as a predictor of what will happen if illegitimate demands are acceded to under pressure.

One difficulty with closest point estimation is its demands upon the memory. This difficulty can be alleviated at only slight cost in potential additional error by forgetting many of the typical cases. It is necessary to recall only a few of the typical cases and all of the unusual cases in order to get most of the benefit of a closest point estimation technique.

In practice, people seem to weight cases differently when they are looking for the closest one. This means that a prominent case may be used as the basis for prediction even though a less prominent case is closer to the current values of the dependent variables. I conjecture that two factors which help account for the prominence assigned to a case by a particular individual are (1) whether the person was a participant in that case and (2) whether the case had important effects. Participation in a case (such as an international crisis) can be either <u>direct</u> (if the person was one of the leaders involved in the crisis) or <u>indirect</u> (if the person was a citizen of one of the countries involved in the crisis). Some corollaries of this conjecture are that people tend to learn little from each other's experience, and little from episodes that did not have important effects. This is not an efficient way to use data, especially when there are only a few cases.

Epistemology

Epistemology deals with the question of how we know what we know. An important aspect of this question is how conclusions are drawn from experience. In the language of belief systems, this is simply the question of which prediction processes are used to derive beliefs from data. In general, this is the same as the problem of hypothesis formation, since each prediction process yields a belief as a function of the data, and this belief can be tested for accuracy against past and future data.

Often a person does not use a single prediction process, but rather he uses a whole sequence of prediction processes, $P = \{p_l\}_{l \in L}$ where now L is the integers.* If one prediction process (l = 1) does not yield a satisfactory prediction with a given set of data, he may go on to a second one (l = 2), and so on. Typically the sequence proceeds to predictions of more and more complex beliefs to account for the data.

---

*Even more often, L is only partially ordered.

Regression techniques, for example, can be thought of as a whole sequence of prediction processes. If a straight line does not account for the data, a quadratic equation might be tried. As more degrees of freedom are used for the extra parameters, fewer remain to estimate the specific values of the parameters.

Recursive causal inference can be thought of as a sequence of prediction processes yielding a sequence of regression equations with different dependent variables. By assuming a hierarchical ordering of the variables and independent error terms, each prediction equation can include as an independent variable the dependent variable of the predicting equation.

Regression uses linear logic, but the problems inherent in selecting a prediction process are perhaps most clear in binary logic. In binary logic each variable can take on one of only two values. Thus it seems that there could not be very many different beliefs. An interesting exercise is to guess how many functions there are from, say, six binary variables into one binary variable. The answer is $(2)^{2^n}$ for n variables in the tail of the function. For n = 6 this is 2^{64}, which is more than 10^{18}--or a billion billion--possible beliefs.

In practice people consider only a few of these beliefs as being "eligible" as results of their prediction process. Given a set of data with six independent variables, a person might look for a function of a given form, such as the conjunction of two of the variables (i.e., $v_k = v_j \cap v_j'$). This is similar to looking for the best linear function in linear logic. There are $\binom{6}{2} =$ 15 ways of selecting two variables from a list of six. Therefore, if a person assumes in advance that the best belief to account for the data is a conjunction of two variables, then there are only 15 rather than a billion billion functions to consider. However, if he assumes that only two variables of the six are relevant, but does not know what the form of the function will be, then there are $2^{2^2} \binom{6}{2} = 16(15) = 240$ possible beliefs.

Concept learning provides an important illustration of the prediction processes people actually use. A set of data is provided (usually sequentially) with a number of dependent variables in the form of attributes (often binary). The dependent variable is a statement of whether the particular case is an exemplar of the concept or not (or in the language of belief systems, whether the value of the concept function in the current case is 1 or 0). There is a finding which is quite well-established about which processes people prefer with binary data (Bruner, Goodnow, Austin, 1956, 237f):

Hypothesis: When using binary logic, the prediction processes that people prefer are conjunctive.

People tend to look for an explanation of the data which takes the form of a belief that the concept in question exists (equals one) when the case has this characteristic and that characteristic and that other characteristic. Even when Harvard students are told that the explanation of the data will be a disjunction (this characteristic or that one), they slip into methods of reasoning and search which are appropriate only to conjunctive concepts.

Bruner, Goodnow, and Austin (1956, 181) make an epistemological point closely related to the hypothesis just cited.

It is characteristic of much scientific thinking to assume at the outset that whatever behaves in a common way does so for a common cause. Common effects have common causes. The disjunctive category is a violation of this classical conception. . . . Perhaps we have learned such rules too well and here lies the origin of our clumsiness with disjunctive concepts.

The observation noted earlier that negative instances of a concept are not as useful to people as positive instances may also be due to people's tendency to use conjunctive rather than disjunctive concepts. This is because negative instances typically provide less information in specifying conjunctions than in specifying disjunctions.

When the data matrix is low (few cases) and wide (many variables), prediction is difficult. In such a case people often employ intermediate concepts to collapse several old variables into one new one. The use of concepts therefore lowers the number of variables that have to be studied. The heads of the concepts can then be regarded as the variables in a new data matrix over the same cases. Thus concepts serve to replace a wide data matrix with a narrower one.

This suggests that there are at least three separate determinants of the predictions a person will make:

(1) His experience (i.e., the data set);

(2) His concepts (i.e., the way he constructs the variables to be examined and to be accounted for); and

(3) His prediction process (i.e., the way he selects a particular kind of function to account for a set of data).

International relations provides an illustration. All three factors are likely to be different for people in different countries, especially the first, then the second, and to a lesser extent the third. No wonder people in different countries make different predictions.

PHASE 4: THE EXPERIMENTER

Instruments

In the first three phases of the model the person was entirely passive. He had beliefs, observations, and predictions, but he had no control over his environment. In Phase 4, the person is allowed some tools with which he can affect his environment.

The manner in which tools can be introduced into the formal model of belief systems is to identify a subset of the variables as instruments. An _instrument_ is any variable whose value in a specific case is under the person's control. Instruments are thus among the observed variables, and they are usually treated as among the independent or exogenous variables.

When some of the independent variables are instruments, the task of finding an accurate belief to explain a set of data moves from mere prediction to the more involved issues of experimental design. The experimental problem is how to set the variables which are under control so that the best record of accuracy is obtained. This in turn requires a measure of accuracy which takes account of the fact that a miss is <u>not</u> as good as a mile. In other words, a measure of the error of a belief is needed which is able to distinguish degrees of error.

<u>Definition</u>: The <u>error</u>, m_{ik}, on the head of a belief, b_k, in a given case i as measured by a given metric, m, is $m_{ik} = m(v_k, b_k(a_{ik}))$.

The meaning of this definition is illustrated for the situation in which there is no error in the following theorem:

<u>Theorem</u>: A belief, b_k, is accurate if and only if $m_{ik} = 0$.

The proof is a simple application of the definition of an accurate belief and the second property of a metric function.

Error is a real number because it is defined by the value of a metric function. Therefore, there is no difficulty comparing errors to each other.

There are at least two different ways of measuring success in using instruments to help derive accurate beliefs. The first method is to establish a criterion for error, and then measure how many cases it takes before a person can consistently predict with no more than this amount of error. The second method is to allow a fixed number of cases for observation, and then measure the total error in a completely different data set. The first method is useful in studying the speed of a learning process, and the second is useful in studying the application of newly learned beliefs to different data. In either case, the error of the process depends both on how well the instruments were used and how adequate the prediction process was for the data at hand. (Error could have been defined and used in the preceding phase [the predictor] but it is only with the introduction of instruments that the questions of experimental design become relevant.)

In the preceding phase of the model, learning had to be passive. However, once a person is allowed some control over the cases he faces, then learning can be active. The person can, for example, hold all but one of his instrumental variables constant in order to try to isolate the effect of that one variable. A procedure such as this would certainly make calculations easier and would also lessen the demands on the memory. The behavior of a person in setting the instrumental variables and in making predictions can be regarded as a strategy.

Concept formation studies have determined which strategies are most efficient for particular purposes, and which strategies are actually used (see Bruner, Goodnow, and Austin, 1956, chs. 4 and 5).

Experiments

The formal theory of experimental design could undoubtedly be incorporated into the fourth phase of belief systems. However, this task will not be undertaken here. One of the principal purposes of such a theory is to specify how to set the instrumental variables in such a way that maximum accuracy of the beliefs can be attained with a fixed number of cases. Obviously, assumptions must be made about the non-instrumental variables and about the prediction process. Once this is done, experimental design becomes analyzable within the context of belief systems.

In actual practice of policy domains, experiments are either common or rare--depending upon the domain. Experiments in modern medicine are common, and the strategies are quite well established. In international relations, national actors rarely experiment, which is to say they rarely decide what to do in a given situation on the basis of what decision will help them learn about their environment for the sake of future accuracy. Instead, each move is based upon current beliefs, with relatively little regard for how instruments can be used to improve the accuracy of beliefs in the future. The major exception is that national actors often make trial moves in order to observe the response of other national actors.

This phase of the model has treated instruments as ways of gaining accurate beliefs. Instruments can also be treated as ways of gaining utility. The next phase of the model deals with that problem.

PHASE 5:   THE DECISION-MAKER

Utility

Utility can be thought of as an index of what a person
wants. He wants utility--by definition. In belief systems,
utility can be represented as just another variable, provided
that the variable is at least partially ordered. To identify
the variable that will be used to represent utility, the notation will be v_u where uϵK. This variable, v_u, is sometimes
called utility, and it is sometimes called the payoff. The notion of utility becomes helpful when something is asserted concerning a person's beliefs about how his utility can be maximized.
Once this is done, analysis can be undertaken to prescribe how
the person should use his instruments to achieve high utility,
and to describe how the person does in fact use his instruments.

The most direct type of belief about utility is a belief
which specifies the exact value of the utility variable for each
possible thing that can happen. The set of things that can happen
can be regarded as a set of variables, called outcomes. If a
coin is being flipped, the two possible outcomes are heads and
tails. Where the coin is a fair one, the expected outcome is a
probability mixture of the two possible outcomes--i.e., 50 percent
heads and 50 percent tails.

In general, a set of outcomes satisfies the conditions
of a probability distribution for each case. Each outcome has
zero or positive probability, and the sum of the probabilities
of the outcomes is one for each case. Such a set can be called
a p-set.

Definition: A set of variables $\{v_j\}_{j \epsilon J'}$ is a p-set (or has
a probability distribution) if $v_j \epsilon R$ for all jϵJ',
and for all iϵI:

$$v_{ij} \geq 0$$

$$\sum_{j \epsilon J'} v_{ij} = 1$$

Notice that a p-set is a probability distribution over a
whole set of variables rather than a single one, as was previously
defined. In terms of the matrix of variables (Figure 6), a p-set
is a horizontal probability distribution, while the probability
of a single variable over a sample is a vertical probability distribution. Let a p-vector mean a vector over a p-set.

Now the definition of a utility function can be introduced.

37

Definition: For $u \varepsilon K$, b_u is a <u>utility function</u> if $T(b_u)$ is a p-set, and $H(b_u)$ is (at least) a partially ordered variable known as utility.

Thus a utility function is a belief about how outcomes affect the payoff. One of the major uses of a belief system is in the use of deduction to determine how to maximize expected utility. Notice that the payoff variable is not necessarily a real number, although the probability of each outcome is a real number. In particular, the values of payoff (or utility) variables may be only partially ordered. This would correspond to an ordinal utility.

If v_u is a real number, then b_u must be a cardinal utility function. There is one type of cardinal utility function which is widely used in studies of decision-making and game theory because it can be constructed from ordinal choices among lotteries over outcomes. This type of utility function might be called a Von Neumann-Morgenstern (VN-M) utility function, because they gave an axiomatic development of it (1947). To define a VN-M utility function, a few new pieces of notation should first be introduced. Let 0 be the set of outcomes which can be directly evaluated--i.e., $0 = T(b_u)$. Then a_0 for $o \varepsilon 0$ is a probability distribution over the outcomes. For example, the flipping of a fair coin yields $a_0 = (.50, .50)$ where $T(b_u) = 0 = \{heads, tails\}$. The occurrence of a specific outcome will be denoted by a prime. Thus o' is a specific outcome, say "heads." Then $a_{o'} = (1, 0)$. In general, the definition of $a_{o'}$ is a vector whose components are all zero except the component corresponding to o', which is one.

Definition: For $v_u \varepsilon R$, b_u is a <u>Von Neumann-Morgenstern utility function</u> if b_u is a utility function such that

$$b_u(a_o) = \sum_{o'} b_u(a_{o'}) v_{o'}.$$

In other words, a VN-M utility function is a belief that the utility of any probability distribution over the outcomes, a_o, is the weighted average of the utilities of the outcomes themselves, $b_u(a_{o'})$, where the weights are the probabilities of a particular outcome occurring, $v_{o'}$.

By definition a VN-M utility function employs a linear logic with respect to probability. This is not to say that the function itself needs to be linear. Consider, for example, a VN-M utility function that is also a simple belief where the tail of the belief is monetary income, m. For m measured in dollars, a specific example might be $b_u(m) = m^3$, which is shown in Figure

8. With this situation a person would prefer to take an even chance of gaining a dollar (Point a) to the certainty of gaining a half dollar (b), but he would also prefer to lose a half dollar (c), to taking an even chance of losing a whole dollar (d).

An important property of a VN-M utility function is that once any two values are known the entire function becomes well-defined. This is like a measure of temperature, which can be defined by two points such as the freezing and boiling point for water. The next theorem expresses this point.

Theorem: If $b_{u'}$ and $b_{u''}$ are VN-M utility functions and $o' \neq o''$, then $b_{u'}(a_{o'}) = b_{u''}(a_{o'})$ and $b_{u'}(a_{o''}) = b_{u''}(a_{o''})$ implies $b_{u'} = b_{u''}$.

Proof: See Luce and Raiffa (1957, ch. 2) for an equivalent demonstration.

Now that utility has been defined, the obvious question is the relationship between utility and choice.

Statistical Decision-Making

Under Certainty

If the outcome variables are all instruments, then the person can be certain about the outcome and about the consequent payoff. This is decision-making under certainty. The problem of choice is trivial because the person need only select the outcome vector which maximizes his expected utility. If he has a VN-M utility function, the best outcome will be $a_{o'}$ for some $o' \varepsilon O$.

Under Risk

To eliminate certainty, the outcomes are not allowed to be instruments. Instead, the outcomes are determined jointly by a set of instruments and a set of unobserved variables. The set of instruments are called "acts," and will be denoted by $R = \{r\}$, with a particular act denoted by r'. The set of unobserved variables are called the "states of natures" (or "states" for short), and will be denoted by $S = \{s\}$, with a particular state denoted by s'. The assumption that the outcome is determined jointly by the act and the state can be expressed easily as a Cartesian product, $O = R \times S$. (Since there will be little need to refer to the whole set of acts as R, there should be no confusion with the same symbol representing the set of real numbers.) A particular outcome is $o' = r' \times s' = (r', s')$. Expressed as a p-vector this is $a_{o'} = a_{r's'}$. The probability that outcome $o' = r's'$

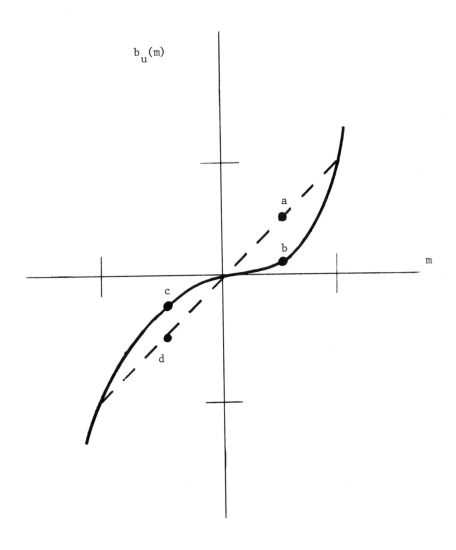

Figure 8. A Nonlinear Utility Function for Money

occurs is simply $v_{o'} = v_{r's'}$. The probability that a particular state, s', occurs can be written as $v_{s'}$. Both the acts and the states are assumed to be p-sets, and this makes the set of outcomes a p-set.

The problem for decision-making under risk is to find the values of the instruments which maximize the expected utility of the outcome when the probabilities of the states are known. This problem can be readily solved if $b_u(a_{r's})$ can be calculated for a general state, s, in terms of the known utility function $b_u(a_0) = b_u(a_{rs})$ and the known probabilities of the particular states, $v_{s'}$. The solution is embodied in the following theorem:

Theorem: If b_u is a VN-M utility function, $b_u(a_{r's}) = \Sigma_{s'} b_u(a_{r's'}) v_{s'}$.

Proof: $b_u(a_{r's}) = \sum_{r's'\varepsilon r' \times S} b_u(a_{r's'}) v_{r's'}$

$= \Sigma_{s'} b_u(a_{r's'}) v_{r's'}$

$= \Sigma_{s'} b_u(a_{r's'}) v_{s'}$.

The last step results from $v_{r's'} = v_{s'}$ for $v_{r'} = 1$.

Under Risk with Experimentation

The next complexity is to assume that although the a priori probabilities of the states are known, there is also an experiment which yields additional information. The experiment has a set of possible outcomes $\{v_e\}_{e\varepsilon E}$. A key assumption is that which outcome of the experiments occurs is a function of which state exists. The experimental outcomes are an observable p-set, but the states are not directly observable. The beliefs about how a given state leads to a given experimental outcome will be denoted $\{b_{e'}(a_s)\}_{e'\varepsilon E}$ and are assumed to be known. The problem is that these beliefs are many-tailed, so that each outcome may be caused by any of the states. However, if the experimental belief functions (about how a particular experimental outcome is a function of the various states) are not all equal, then something new can be inferred about the probabilities of the states. When this is done the problem is reduced to one of decision-making under risk.

In the notation of belief systems, the problem of decision-making with a fixed experiment is to calculate the expected utility of an act given the experimental outcome $b_u(a_{r'}, s|e')$ based upon (1) a set of beliefs each specifying the probability that a

41

given experimental outcome will result if a given state actually occurs--i.e., $b_{e'}(s') = p(e'|s')$; (2) the a priori probabilities of each state, $v_{s'}$; and (3) the VN-M utility function on each outcome, defined by an act-state pair--i.e., $b_u(a_{r's'})$. The answer is embodied in the following theorem:

Theorem: For b_u, a VN-M utility function,

$$b_u(a_{r'}, s|e') = \sum_{s'} b_u(a_{r's'}) \left[\frac{b_{e'}(a_{s'})v_{s'}}{\sum_{s''} b_{e'}(a_{s''})v_{s''}} \right]$$

Proof: $b_u(a_{r'}, s|e') = \sum_{s'} b_u(a_{r's'})v_{s'|e'}$ by definition. The next step is the use of Bayes theorem to express the probability, $v_{s'|e'}$, of a state occurring when a given experimental outcome occurs.

This theorem allows the specification of a decision rule. For each experimental outcome, e', there is an act, r', which maximizes the expected utility, $b_u(a_{r'}, s|e')$. This defines the decision rule as a function from experimental outcomes into acts.

If there is a whole set of experiments available, the decision rule can be made to include not only the choice among actions, but also the choice among experiments (Luce and Raiffa, 1957, 313-6).

Under Uncertainty

The problem of decision-making under uncertainty is just like the problem of decision-making under risk except that there is no a priori probability distribution of the states. There is no completely satisfactory answer to the question of which act to select if all that is known is the utility function on act-state pairs.

An example of one of the partially satisfactory rules is the maximin criterion. The idea is that with each act, r', there exists a worst possible state (or states), s', such that $\{b_u(a_{r's'})\}_{s'\varepsilon S}$ is minimized. This value of the expected utility can be thought of as the security level for the act, r'. A pessimistic person would seek to pick the act that had the highest security level. The expected payoff would then be at least $\max_{r'} \min_{s'} b_u(a_{r's'})$. Frequently, the object considered in the literature is loss or negative utility rather than gain. In that case, the pessimistic person wishes to minimize his maximum loss $(\min_r, \max_s, (-b_u(a_{r's'})))$, and the criterion is known as minimax.

Empirical Decision-Making

Satisficing

Statistical decision-making may be a normatively valid approach, but it asks a great deal of any person who tries to employ it. Several authors have described decision-making procedures which are not quite as demanding and which seem to be better descriptions of how people actually make decisions. To the extent that these procedures can be formalized, one can try to state them in the language of belief systems.

A major example of a less demanding decision-making procedure is Simon's satisficing (1957). As before, there are instruments which can be manipulated to choose an act, and as before, an outcome can be represented as a vector over a set of outcome variables, $\{v_j\}_{j \in J'}$. These variables are assumed to be real numbers. The form of belief about how the outcome variables affect the payoff variable is key to the process.

Definition: A satisficing belief is a belief

$$b_c: a_o \to v_u \text{ for } a_o \underset{j \in J'}{\Longleftarrow}$$

where v_j is a real number and there exists a set of real valued constants $\{k_j\}_{j \in J'}$, such that

(1) $b_c(a_o) = 1$ if $v_j \geq k_j$ for all $j \in J'$
(2) $b_c(a_o) = 0$ otherwise.

The constants, $\{k_j\}_{j \in J'}$, can be thought of as aspiration levels. Then any outcome which meets or exceeds the aspiration levels for each of the outcome variables is as good as any other. The person merely has to search through his acts until he finds one that yields one of these satisficing outcomes.

To use this process a person does not need probability estimates of anything. In particular, his set of outcome variables need not be a p-set, and thus the satisficing function need not be a strict utility function. The person also does not need to be able to distinguish his preferences for different outcomes except for the one distinction of whether the outcome is good enough on each of the separate outcome variables. Such a process is clearly an application of the notion of "bounded rationality."

Of course, the satisficing procedure leaves unanswered a number of questions. How, for example, are the aspiration levels set? And how does the search procedure work? These questions have been the focus of a considerable body of empirical studies in both the laboratory and the field. The interested reader is referred to Cyert and March (1963, ch. 3) for a good discussion with emphasis on decision-making in organizations.

Selective Attention to Goals

Cyert and March (1963) have extended the satisficing notion. In their studies of decision-making in the context of an organization, they found that people often treat the variables that determine the outcome as if they were subgoals. In other words, people try to maximize each of the variables in the tail of the satisficing function. Typically they are not able to maximize them all at once, so they do it sequentially. This decision-making technique can be called "selective attention to goals."

The problem with this procedure of bounded rationality is that the outcome variables are typically functionally related. Thus, the setting of instruments to maximize one of the outcome variables (or subgoals as they would then be called) would also affect the other outcome variables. If one of these other outcome variables fell below its aspiration level, then the instruments would have to be used to improve that outcome variable. If the index of cases is thought of as the time dimension, then the same instruments might be used to adjust a different subgoal in each sequential time period.*

Cognitive Dissonance

Another area of study of the empirical decision-making process is concerned with what happens after a decision is reached. While justice cannot be done to this literature in a short space, one of its major findings can be stated succinctly in the language of belief systems:

Hypothesis: After r' is chosen, b_u is changed such that $(b_u(a_{r's}) - b_u(a_{rs}))$ is increased for all $s \varepsilon S$ and for all acts $r' \neq r$.

---

*The general case of behavioral feedback can be handled in the theoretical framework by means of cycles of observation, prediction, choice, outcome, and new observation. The beliefs are modified in each cycle as the sample of observation grows larger. I wish to thank Zoltan Domotor for emphasizing the need to consider feedback.

PHASE 5: THE DECISION-MAKER

Once an act is chosen, the potential payoff of other choices sets up what has been called "cognitive dissonance" (Festinger, 1957). The finding is that a person tends to like the result of his choice (relative to other choices) even more after the decision than before it.

This finding bears a certain resemblance to the finding of the tendency toward cognitive balance mentioned in Phase 1. Together, these two hypotheses--cognitive dissonance and cognitive balance--have inspired a great deal of experimentation and analysis. Citing some of the recent survey books and articles will demonstrate this point: Abelson et al. (1968), Insko (1967), Kiesler et al. (1969), and McGuire (1969).

PHASE 6: THE STRATEGIST

Formal Game Theory

Definition of a Game

The first five phases of the mathematical model of belief systems dealt with the beliefs, observations, and decisions of a single person. The task for the sixth phase of the model is to extend the model to more than one person.

The method of extension is again the introduction of a new index set and subscript. Let H be a set of people, and let $h\epsilon H$ be one of these people. Then a whole set of belief systems can be described, one for each person, giving a (B_h, V_h) for each $h\epsilon H$.

The most important literature about how people make decisions when there are other people to be taken account of is game theory. In essence, formal game theory treats the problem of decision-making under uncertainty, but with a new twist. The twist is that the state of nature for one person is determined by the acts of the other people. Thus the outcome for each person is determined jointly by the acts of all the people. To make things manageable, everyone is assumed to have a Von Neumann-Morgenstern utility function, and everyone is assumed to know the utility functions of all the others. The definition of a game follows from this description.

Definition: A <u>game</u>, G, is a set of belief systems, $\{B_h, V_h\}_{h\epsilon H}$, each with a set of beliefs, $\{b_{uh}\}_{h'\epsilon H} \subset B_h$ such that:

(1) These beliefs are VN-M utility functions $b_{uh}: a_{oh} \rightarrow v_{uh}$, <u>and</u>

(2) The tails of the beliefs are defined by $a_{oh} = a_{rh} \times a_{sh}$ for $r\epsilon R_h$, $s\epsilon S_h$, where R_h and S_h are p-sets of instruments and states

for $h\epsilon H$ and $a_{sh} = \bigtimes_{h'\epsilon H - h} a_{rh'}$.

Notice that each person's beliefs include the utility functions of all the others. This is an assumption of complete information, and needless to say is a feature of a normative theory rather than a descriptive theory. The first condition in the definition asserts that the utility functions are all VN-M utility functions. The second condition asserts that a person's outcome is determined by his own choice and the state

46

of nature, while the state of nature is determined by the choices of others through their acts.

Types of Games

The task for formal game theory is to specify what each person should do with his instruments. Once this is done, the strategy choice, a_{rh}, is determined for each $h \varepsilon H$. This determines all of the outcome for each person and thus the payoff for each person.

There is no need to review the specific solutions offered by game theory since they are so widely known and available. However, it may be helpful to indicate how the language of belief systems can be used to describe a few of the fundamental distinctions in game theory.

Definition: A strategy, a_{rh}, is a pure strategy if $v_{r'h} = 1$ for some $r' \varepsilon R_h$. In general, a_{rh} is a mixed strategy.

Definition: An n-person game is a game with size (H) = n. A two-person game is an n-person game where n = 2.

Definition: A zero-sum game is a game such that there exists for each $h \varepsilon H$ a $b_{u'h}$ which is equivalent* to b_{uh} which gives for all sets of possible outcomes,

$$\{a_{oh}\}_{h \varepsilon H}, \quad \sum_{h \varepsilon H} b_{u'h}(a_{oh}) = 0.$$

Definition: A non-zero-sum game is a game that is not a zero-sum game.

Von Neumann and Morgenstern (1944) demonstrate that every two-person zero-sum game has an unequivocal solution in mixed strategies--namely, the minimax strategy for each player. Since then a great deal of effort has gone into studying what could be said about games with more than two players and games that are not zero-sum. For the interested reader, an excellent introduction and critical survey is the one by Luce and Raiffa (1957).

---

*The arbitrariness of the zero and unit point of a VN-M utility function was noted in a preceding theorem. With allowance for this arbitrariness, two utility functions can be said to be equivalent if one is a positive linear transformation of the other.

Experimental Games

Laboratory experiments can be set up to approximate the conditions of a formal game. The subjects can be told that they have range of choices, and they can be shown how the outcomes will be determined jointly by their choice and by the choices of others. Then the subjects can be observed as they make their actual choices of strategies. The task of experimental gaming is to understand how people actually behave in specific gaming situations. The situations are designed to allow (in idealized form) choice behavior such as bargaining, cooperation, competition, double-cross, and alliance formation.

One problem is that while the outcomes can be specified, the utility functions can not. A common assumption is that when small amounts of money are involved a person's utility payoff is a linear function of his monetary reward. Thus if m_h is the amount of money person h wins in a game, the assumption is that $b_{uh}(a_{oh}) = km_h$ for some real constant, k. Curiously enough, people do not seem to act according to this assumption. Instead, their actual utility functions take into account not only their own monetary gains, but also the monetary gains of the other player (or players). Most people play competitively in a broad variety of settings: they are willing to sacrifice at least a little monetary gain if it means less monetary gain for others. This suggests the following definition and hypothesis which will serve as an example of the value of experimental games.

Definition: A competitive person, h', is a person whose utility function has a negative partial differential with respect to monetary gains by other people--i.e., $\frac{\partial b_{uh'}}{\partial m_h} < 0$ for $h \neq h'$.

Hypothesis: Everyone is a competitive person.

Like other hypotheses in this paper, this one is stated in a form so general that it goes considerably beyond the available evidence. Nevertheless, among the many specific findings of experimental game theory, the competitiveness of the subjects is one of the most ubiquitous. Fortunately for the subjects, even competitive people can learn to cooperate with each other if the direct monetary gains are large enough to compensate for the pleasure of doing better than the other fellow.

Both formal game theory and experimental gaming take as givens the beliefs about how acts and states determine outcomes and how outcomes determine payoffs. Of course, the origin of beliefs such as these from old beliefs, from observations, from prediction processes, and from experiments is exactly what the first four phases of the belief system model are designed to handle.

WHY BOTHER?

The framework for a general theory of cognition and choice has now been presented. Because of its formal character, the framework is not easy to learn. Readers may well ask, "Why bother?" I would answer as follows.

1. The framework illuminates some of the tasks a person must be able to perform if he is to act intelligently. For example, it analyzes the nature of the prediction task and explains why people dealing with international relations often resort to historical analogies rather than rely on more sophisticated prediction techniques (pp. 30-32).

2. The framework enhances the value of many different bodies of knowledge by showing the role each can play within a broader study of cognition and choice. The enhancement is achieved in several ways. By relating literatures from different fields dealing with the same task, the framework shows how the insights of one approach can be applied to the problems of another approach. An example is the application of circuit theory and statistical causal inference to cognitive logics (p. 10). By relating descriptive and normative literatures concerned with the same task, the framework can be used to generate advice to improve performance, as in concept learning (pp. 32-34). By relating literatures that deal with different tasks, the framework can show how the foundations of one field can sometimes be based on the conclusions of another field, as when the utility function assumed to exist in game theory is derived from the structure of a belief system (p. 37).

3. The framework can help advance the study of cognition and choice. Parsimony promotes synergism. In other words, the more our knowledge is integrated into meaningful patterns, the more readily we can see things we could not see before. The framework itself suggests new questions which need to be answered with new empirical studies. For example, the analysis of the role of belief systems as cognitive maps (pp. 6-16) suggests questions about the structural properties of the cognitive maps used by actual decision-makers. More important, the framework suggests how an empirical study (such as Axelrod, forthcoming) can answer this type of question.

A framework for a general theory is not as useful as a general theory, but it helps.

BIBLIOGRAPHY

Abelson, R.P., and Rosenberg, M.J. "Symbolic Psycho-logic: A Model of Attitude Cognition," Behavioral Science, 3 (1958), 1-13.

Abelson, R.P., et al., eds. Theories of Cognitive Consistency: A Sourcebook. Chicago: Rand McNally, 1968.

Axelrod, Robert. "Psycho-Algebra: A Mathematical Theory of Cognition and Choice with an Application to the British Eastern Committee in 1918," Papers of the Peace Research Society (International), forthcoming.

Blalock, Hubert M., Jr. Causal Inference in Nonexperimental Research. Chapel Hill: University of North Carolina Press, 1961.

Bruner, J.S., Goodnow, J.J., and Austin, G.A. A Study of Thinking. New York: Wiley, 1956.

Busaker, Robert, and Saaty, Thomas. Finite Graphs and Networks. New York: McGraw-Hill, 1965.

Coombs, Clyde H. A Theory of Data. New York: Wiley, 1964.

Copi, Irving. Symbolic Logic. New York: Macmillan, 1954.

Cyert, Richard, and March, James G. A Behavioral Theory of the Firm. Englewood Cliffs, N.J.: Prentice-Hall, 1963.

Eriksen, C.W., and Wechsler, H. "Some Effects of Experimentally Induced Anxiety upon Discrimination Behavior," Journal of Abnormal and Social Psychology, 51 (1955), 458-463.

Festinger, L. A Theory of Cognitive Dissonance. Evanston, Ill.: Row, Peterson, 1957.

Garner, Wendell R. Uncertainty and Structure as Psychological Concepts. New York: Wiley, 1962.

Giese, Paula. "The Logic of 'Symbolic Psycho-logic,'" Behavioral Science, 12 (1967), 391-395.

Harary, Frank, Norman, Robert Z., and Cartwright, Dorwin. Structural Models: An Introduction to the Theory of Directed Graphs. New York: Wiley, 1966.

Heider, F. "On the Measurement of Structural Valence," Behavioral Science, 4 (1959), 316-323.

Hovland, C.I. "A 'Communications Analysis' of Concept Learning," Psychological Review, 59 (1952), 461-472.

Hunt, Earl B. Concept Learning: An Information Processing Problem. New York: Wiley, 1962.

Insko, Chester. Theories of Attitude Change. New York: Appleton-Century-Crofts, 1967.

Kiesler, Charles, Callins, Barry, and Miller, Norman. Attitude Change. New York: Wiley, 1969.

Lambert, R.M. "An Examination of the Consistency Characteristics of Abelson and Rosenberg's 'Symbolic Psycho-logic,'" Behavioral Science, 11 (1966), 126-130.

Luce, R. Duncan, and Raiffa, Howard. Games and Decisions. New York: Wiley, 1957.

McGuire, William. "The Nature of Attitude and Attitude Change" in Gardner Lindzey and Elliot Aronson, eds., The Handbook of Social Psychology. Vol. 3, Second Edition, 136-314. Reading, Mass.: Addison-Wesley, 1969.

Miller, G.A. "The Magical Number Seven, Plus or Minus Two," Psychological Review, 63 (1956), 81-97.

Osgood, C.E., and Tannenbaum, P.H. "The Principle of Congruity in the Prediction of Attitude Change," Psychological Review, 62 (1955), 42-55.

Peizer, David. "On Critiques of 'Symbolic Psycho-Logic,'" Behavioral Science, 14 (1969), 40-46.

Simon, Herbert. Models of Man. New York: Wiley, 1957.

Stinchcombe, Arthur L. Constructing Social Theories. New York: Harcourt, Brace and World, 1968.

Von Neumann, John, and Morgenstern, Oskar. Theory of Games and Economic Behavior. Princeton: Princeton University Press, 1944 (First Edition), 1947 (Second Edition).

INDEX OF TERMS*

Accuracy of a belief, 20
Accuracy of a prediction process, 28
Act, 39
Active learning, 36
Alternation-minimal set of beliefs, 15
Aspiration level, 43
Average uncertainty, 22
Axiom, 5
Balance, 14, 45
Belief, 5
Belief system, 6
Binary logic, 11
Case, 18
Causal inference, 10, 33
Cause, 6
Certainty, decision-making under, 39
Channel capacity, 24
Circuit theory, 10
Closest point estimation, 30
Cognitive balance, 14, 45
Cognitive consistency, 14
Cognitive dissonance, 45
Competitive person, 48
Concept, 17
Concept formation, 16, 33
Conditional uncertainty, 26
Conjunction, 11
Contingent uncertainty, 23
Data, 18
Decision-making, statistical, 39
  Under certainty, 39
  Under risk, 39
  Under risk with experimentation, 41
  Under uncertainty, 42
Dependent variable, 28
Digraph, 7
Disjunction, 11
Effect, 6
Epistemology, 32
Error, 35

---

*Note: The page references indicate where the term is defined or specified.

*